MOVING WITH HEAVEN

GOD IS

THE PROPHETIC WORSHIPER'S HANDBOOK   VOL II

James Vincent

MOVING WITH HEAVEN: GOD IS THE PROPHETIC WORSHIPER'S HANDBOOK VOL. II

©2017 James Vincent III

Printed in USA

ISBN-13: 978-0-9986413-0-0
ISBN-10: 0998641300

4

Contents

Introduction

God is majestic. God is unfathomable. He is beyond our realm of understanding, incomprehensible to our earthly mind. True to the praises that have been declared throughout the ages, his glory is greater than we can imagine. With a mutter, he created the light; with but a thought, his words formed the intricate detailed expanse of the entire universe.

How marvelous is this God of gods!!! Can you think of one being in this world who is worthy to be compared in any way to him? What is impossible for him? Oh God, that you would reveal what we don't see; that you'd cause us to comprehend the depth of our weakness and foolishness so that we can just turn and see that you are the power above, below, within, and around all that you command us to do. We bless your holy, almighty name!

John 1:1-5

In the beginning was the Word, and the Word was with God, and the Word was God. He was in the beginning with God. All things came into being through Him, and without Him not even one thing came into being that has come into being. In Him was life, and the life was the light of men. And the light shines in the darkness, and the darkness did not overtake it.

Understanding that he is, and that all things came into being through him, and that there was not a thing that was made that wasn't made without him is a basis of the power of the saints of God. As worshipers, we know that through the sacrifice and spilled blood of Jesus, we enter in to the richness of his promise when we believe and confess (Romans 10:9). We become quickened by his life as his breath comes to dwell inside of us. We are no longer powerless, but have the vastness of all that he is and has ever been, available to us. When we are in line with what he is saying and doing, and operating in the faith that believes in the totality of him, how can we be stopped?

I began by declaring the wonderful praises of God. One

reason I did that was because it seems that we sometimes forget who it is that empowers us. We act like we are having to depend solely on our own strength in our endeavors, as if there is anything we can accomplish for him by our efforts. Sure, without faith it's impossible to please God, but faith here is about making known through your actions in whom you believe, not about making something happen. We have become very mixed up about where the power comes from; and although we might SAY that all power comes from him, our actions and the state of our heart speak forth an entirely different thing.

What does this have to do with prophetic worship? Everything. The FIRST thing a prophet has to understand about prophecy is not *how to prophesy*, but that there is *a greater one speaking*. Without realizing that, one can become nothing more than a soothsayer or fortune teller, because it's not about the originator, it's about the prophecy... and ultimately it becomes about the person prophesying. When we worship, when we prophesy, we must be careful not to lose our objective, which is and should always be to bring glory to God. We fall into the trap of methods-- and even divination-- when we don't make God the center.

I quoted the first few verses of the gospel of John. As we read those verses and further on, we discover that although he walked among those who SHOULD have known him, they neither recognized nor accepted him. This is the danger we are in as worshipers-- not only those who lead in worship (dancers, singers, musicians, etc.) but all who call themselves worshipers of God. This causes us to revert to the devices of our own thoughts and strength, and we find ourselves at complete enmity with God. This causes an epidemic of powerlessness.

The passage in John goes on to say that those who RECEIVED him were given POWER to become children of God. In our earthly, western (for many of us) mindset, the word "receive" can be reduced to mean to accept as good, or to welcome. While it does mean those things, it's also a picture of taking inside of you the totality of something, allowing yourself to be overcome by it so that you become one with it. It essentially becomes a part of you. Without this, we are just like the Pharisees who Jesus condemned for not knowing God, yet thought they did. In this book I want to emphasize to worshipers the importance of knowing and recognizing God; that we become more than spectacles of talent, skill, and learnedness, but show forth the glory of the one who is full of power.

Hosanna!!! Blessed is he who comes in the name of the Lord!

I. Return to Focus

A worship leader friend of mine once told me a story of a run-in with another church leader. This leader somehow expressed to him that being a worship leader was like a low-level position in the church, as though one should be working his way up to being a pastor or bishop or something. I immediately wanted to vomit. Not because I'm biased as a worshiper, but because this leader was a classic example of why the church is in the state it's in! We have become so focused on everything except what truly matters. In many ways we have abandoned the simplicity of the message of his love, grace, and power, and turned it into a throne-building, man-centered, scholarly, powerless circus of lifelessness. It's a whitewashed tomb.

Singers, dancers, musicians, and those who help facilitate worship should all endeavor to hear the voice of God, as was expressed in the first book, *Moving With Heaven*. Not only should we desire to hear his voice, but we should desire his heart to be expressed in every moment. If you are a worshiper, (leader or not) you hold a very special position. You are being entrusted as an "atmosphere facilitator", and let's face it-- if you're not doing a good job, it's felt. That's why it's imperative that we get to know the heart of God; then "good job" will simply mean that you are fully submitted to God in every moment of your leadership. It becomes only about glorifying him and moving with him.

Where has our focus been? I'll let you make that list of distractions for yourself, but it's time to shift our minds away from the mechanics of what we do and onto the reason we are doing it. Here are some practical questions you can ask yourself moving forward:

Who is the lord to me, and in what ways has he revealed himself to me?

Who does the lord want to be to me?

Who does he want to be to everyone else?

How much of who he is do I really believe?

Of course, you can ask yourself more questions than these, but I felt like these were the most simple and pertinent to get to the heart of the issue. Peter had a revelation of who Jesus was, (Matthew 16) but apparently there was still enough unbelief in his heart to cause him to deny the lord three times on the eve of the crucifixion. If we are going to show forth his power, we must challenge ourselves with these kinds of questions! Other good questions are: Do I truly love him? Am I willing to look like a fool for him?

You see, worship and sound are so much more than what the church seems to perceive today. We don't often equate the songs we sing to an actual person with whom we are relating-- thus we negate the depth of its deeper spiritual reality. If we saw it this way, I don't believe we would treat it quite as common as we tend to. Getting real with ourselves about what we believe should eventually lead us to a crossroads where we must decide to either fully receive all that he is, or completely reject him. I have determined to know him, love him, and receive all of him. As a result, I perceive him more and more as I worship, and consequently, when I minister.

Have you felt that while you're worshiping, you're a bit boxed in? as if there is some threshold you desire to cross, but you just can't seem to get there? I've been there. Our problem, again, might be that we don't have a true revelation of whom it is we're worshiping. I find that every time I stop "trying" to worship, and simply communicate with my lord, I connect to him. Then I begin to see, hear, feel, or discern whatever he may want me to. I begin to know him more deeply by the spirit. Sing this with me:

> *"Turn your eyes upon Jesus; look full in his wonderful face*
> *And the things of earth grow strangely dim*
> *In the light of his glory and grace."*

> *"I turn my eyes upon you, Lord, to look full in your wonderful face*
> *Let the things of this earth grow strangely dim*
> *In the light of your glory and grace."*

Sing this (or create your own song to sing) over and over in order to get your heart in a place of sole focus on him. Determine to remember why you came to desire him; why you praise him. Then minister to him.

Dance outside of the spotlight, where no one sees, extending every movement to the Lord in thankfulness and humility. Play on your instrument, offering every note from your heart to his throne. Don't seek anything except to give him what he is worth, because he is worthy.

When we receive all that he is and we recognize his worth, suddenly our worth increases. Remember the worshiper, David, who was hired by Saul as a minstrel to subside the evil spirit he was being tormented by. We know the story of David, who worshiped God in the field while tending sheep, before he ever had a platform. Suddenly, he was chosen to come before the king and minister to him through sound. He was so blessed by the Lord that Saul made sure he stayed with him wherever he went, making David his armor bearer and having him on call to play his instrument.

Sometimes, when I'm leading in worship and simply glorifying God, I don't physically feel or even sense anything. In fact, sometimes I just want to go home and watch a movie, or take a nap, or eat pizza. But I know that it is worth the lying down of my flesh to see him glorified. Then afterwards, I get all sorts of invitations to come and train teams in worship, people asking for mentorship, and others are even drawn to sow seed into my life. It's like my worth increases simply because I offer God his just due.

I should add that I endeavor to worship with a pure heart, and not for any gain or benefit except to know that I'm pleasing him. Taking this consistently bowed position in worship removes the mentality of the "church building", because we endeavor to honor and glorify him wherever we go. This is what we need to see in our worshipers-- the desire to show him forth in every atmosphere, whether we are leading on stage or at a playground. What makes us prophetic is that we are ready to recognize him and what he is doing, then manifest it in the earth realm.

A true prophet has his ear tuned to the lord, not to revelation. Even diviners are tuned to revelation, as it doesn't matter where their supernatural knowledge comes from (after all is said and done). God is calling forth a priesthood from out of the ashes of Christiandom that will minister to him, as Zadok of the tribe of Levi. (Ezekiel 44-- read the entire chapter). Those who are not lured by the things that suck the church into lukewarmness or cause them to seek things outside of their dependence on his faithfulness and power, but keep their hearts bowed and dedicated to the Lord are whom he is searching for. It's those people he desires to show himself mighty through. (2 Chronicles 16:8-9) Are you one of those people?

If not, you can choose to be right now. Whether you are an apostle or bishop, a banker or a toilet cleaner, it's not your held earthly position that makes you anything. The greatest in the kingdom is the one whose heart is set to serve. The one who is exalted is the one who doesn't seek exaltation. The one who is mighty is the one whose heart is completely towards the Lord. We turn our eyes upon you, Lord. You don't glory in the things that man glories in; position, titles, accolades, degrees and such-- you are a holy God, and we set our face, our mind, our heart to please you, to love what you love and to hate what you hate.

Amen.

II. God is All

One of the things I run into often when leading worship is the fact that many people are very focused on the technical side of their talent/skill and not the prophetic side (or *revelation* side). I acknowledge that there is an aspect to song leading that is technical. I won't even talk about playing or singing on pitch, or just keeping a simple rhythm (although God is outside of that, too-- I know, I just blew. your. mind.). But then, there is a side that is moving with the mood of the spirit. We can't be afraid to move in the moment. I'll give you an example.

Let's take the song, "Revelation Song", by Jennie Lee Riddle. Most of us who know this song know that it's a pretty powerful song. So the band learns it, and because they are good musicians, they get it to sound just like the recording, or at least somewhat close. Or maybe not just like the recording, because, hey... they're original, and they've got to make it their own. Whatever road they took, they've got it down fairly well. We are now playing the song, and we get to the part, "Filled with wonder, awestruck wonder, at the mention of your name..." and here comes the lord, ready to emphasize something in the atmosphere. "Oh, this is gonna be big," he says, "because they are about to get a real picture of the power of my name!" I, as the leader, discern this powerful moment, and I'm ready to submit and play my part to cause the sound to become conducive to the move of God's spirit... I can just feel the bigness of the moment, and everything in me is anticipating what the Lord is about to do in the room! The Spirit is stirred! I am so stirred!!! It's coming. People are about to be delivered of unbelief in this room. Someone is about to truly see God for the first time. Here comes the "JESUS YOUR NAME IS POWER!!!" part... I sing it with all I have--

Yet the band just plays it like they always do.

There is no change, no adjusting to what heaven is wanting to release at that specific time. This happens quite often, and it's one reason, if any of you reading this has ever seen me lead, I run around the stage like a crazed maniac sometimes-- I'm making an effort to communicate in some way how I'm hearing the sound of the Lord coming forth in the moment. Whether I'm jumping up and down, stomping my feet, or swaying from side to side, I lead to cause the team to flow with me as I flow with heaven. An element I do my best to express whenever I share on this subject is: don't simply think "music", think "sound."

Think of music as an avenue for the sound. Think of sound as the part that really needs to be heard, because honestly, God can use anything to convey his sound. Sound is an embodiment of what is being released into the earth. It is such a powerful tool that we often overlook or relegate to pre-message entertainment. Yet, God's voice is described as "the sound of many waters" (Ezekiel 43:2, Revelation 1:15); he thundered from Sinai (Exodus 19:16); he spoke to Elijah in a still, small, voice (1 Kings 19:11-12). In these scriptures, it was more than just the fact that he was speaking-- it was also about the sound he was using to convey his message. In 1 Kings, it was clear that the Lord was not in the wind, the earthquake, or the fire; yet Elijah was intent on hearing the Voice, whichever way it would come. Sound can also be a weapon, as we see more than once in the scriptures. When we gather, we must acknowledge the sound that the Lord may want to convey through us or someone else.

Now that we've established the importance of sound

over music, let's make another thing clear-- God IS the sound. Before we begin to try and break down what sound does, what sound is, how to do it, and blah blah blah, we have to know that God is in all that he does. And that is enough. Don't get caught up in why something is or isn't, or how something is happening, or whatever. When he uses you as a connection from his throne to the ground where you're standing, he knows exactly what he's doing. A humble approach to releasing the sound is the best approach. Can you explain the technicalities of why Jesus used mud and saliva to restore a blind man's sight? If you can, I can already tell you that you've wasted your time trying to figure it out. *HE HEALED A BLIND MAN USING METHODS OUTSIDE OF OUR REASONING.* Worship him because he is beyond. Let his sound carry you beyond so that you can show forth his beyond-ness as well. Let go of the need to understand everything, and just submit to his leading. Joshua probably could not logically explain how the walls of Jericho fell after they shouted and blew trumpets, except to say, "Holy is the Lord who was, is, and is to come!"

Sound him forth when you worship, if in fact you desire to see him perform what only he can perform. He IS healing. He IS power. He IS vindicator. Give him room to manifest himself beyond our understanding of who we think he is. If you let him, he'll continually blow your mind! When he is lifted up, the Lord has declared that he will draw all men to him.

On a side note, it's not *bad* to study and know some of the revelations on sound; as a matter of fact, it can prove to be very useful in some situations. There is wonder to be had in discovering many of the finer details within this subject. Many times, God in his sovereignty will reveal certain mysteries concerning what he wants us to know. Just know that gaining this knowledge is not a prerequisite to moving prophetically with heaven.

I talked in the first book about prophesying by faith. Sometimes you may see or discern something in the spirit. Let's say, for example, you see fire (by the spirit), and you hear in your mind either an intensity, or maybe a quietness that could help convey the sound that accompanies what you see. Take a step in that direction by just doing SOMETHING. Trust that the Lord will see your faith and begin to move in the way you believe you've already seen. A fellow worshiper asked me once, "How do you move into actual prophecy while you are leading? I find it hard for me because I become unsure of myself." I told him that the only way to overcome that fear is to simply do whatever it is we are afraid to do. The enemy will keep us under his control if we don't start demonstrating faith on some level. Jesus said that even with the faith of a *mustard seed*, we can speak to a mountain and watch it fall into the sea. Do you realize how strong and powerful a simple act of faith is?

Faith in God is a huge key on any level of ministry. This worship leader's problem was that his eyes were on himself, and therefore could not see the gracious doorway of opportunity to take that leap of faith. Now understand, moving in presumption is another problem many prophetic people have to be careful of, but when you *never* demonstrate your faith, you will never experience the power behind that faith. Once you begin to practice, and you take that FIRST step of faith, you are already on the path to maturing in knowing when God is ready to speak a particular thing and when it might not be the right time. God is big. We have to see that. When our heart is solely to bring him glory, his glory will manifest. Just open your mouth. Do *something*. Don't let pride (masquerading as insecurity or humility) block you from partnering with the Spirit of God.

I have literally fought myself sometimes when the time came to operate on that level of faith. I recall a time that as I worshiped, I began to see by the spirit that a woman had fire in her belly, and that the lord was going to settle that fire. I didn't want to say that. Most Christians *want* fire in their bellies! Here I am, wanting to quench it.

I finally overcame that hesitation and I prophesied over her what I saw. There. Faith in action. The lady thanked me for the prayer and went her way. I didn't know if the word was true or not, but I believed God enough that he would somehow confirm it to her. It was only up to me to hear his word and show my faith in him by obeying. The pastor came up to me afterwards and whispered to me, "She wouldn't want to admit this to you, but she has had serious complications in her digestive system. We've been believing for her healing. So just know-- that was an accurate word."

Since then, I have sung the prophetic song of the lord over nations, and in a matter of a few weeks or even days, seen that word fulfilled... sometimes even in a few minutes. Then there are some words that have yet to be fulfilled. The lord is ready to sound his sound through us, if only we'd be willing and obedient. Stop looking at yourself, and trust the greater one who is living inside of you!

He is living in you, right?

Be a conduit

A concept I'll be reiterating is the fact that *God is an actual person*. When he said, "Let us create man in our image," he didn't create us as something intangible, without form, without emotion, etc. We seem to have related to God on a level of something that we *do*, or as a *thing*; but not as someone we are personally relating to. We even relate to him sometimes on a scholarly level. People say they know God because they've read about him. They went to bible school, they've read the bible from front to back 50 times, and can even sometimes perform miracles and prophesy. But many of those same people could not tell you what God is truly doing in a specific moment, or how he feels about specific situation without reverting to their brain-learned knowledge. He is a real person who is still speaking today. Here's one for you: Moses healed the waters at with a piece of tree (Exodus 15), yet Elisha healed the waters with salt (2 Kings 2). Which one is God's way? Is it possible that you have to know him beyond the written word? The written word is extremely important, and it should draw us more and more into him. Hopefully, per the instructions from the first book, you've already begun studying the scriptures; but don't use it as a crutch or replacement for the desire to know the person of God in a deeper way.

You are like a connection, or conduit, between heaven and earth if you allow yourself to be. The same way God can use a donkey to speak, he can use anybody. But I want to be intentional about partnering with the person of God. I want him to call me "friend". Being known as a great worship leader or prophet, apostle, minister, or whatever means nothing to me, and it shouldn't to you if you truly want to move alongside the one who made it possible to call yourself a redeemed son of his covenant. When I sound his sound, I know that I am acting as a representative of his mighty voice in the earth. "Oh, that was POWERful!" some people say, or, "Great word you prophesied!" Well, I'm just a conduit. It was God's voice you heard through me.

He's the powerful one; he's the great one. I've chosen to be ready to hear him, walk with him, learn the person of him, and let my faith speak what I believe.

And I believe he is all of everything, and he makes his sound through me.

III.

Breaking Religious Patterns of Worship

Before delving into this subject, I think the concept of religion here needs to be defined. The bible gives a definition of true and undefiled religion in James 1:27. Religion in and of itself is not bad, if the heart of God is evident and not mixed with all kinds of other junk that makes it indistinguishable from the world. When people put their ways and methods above the desire of God, however, or don't care to receive all of who God is, they fall prey to what's been labeled as a *religious spirit*. The religious spirit blinds us from seeing the purity of the lord; from breathing in the essence of his being. It makes the mind bigger than God. It loves to do the same thing, the same way, over and over and over. It only feels comfortable when it does things its way, and doesn't want to be stretched to discover or learn to flow in the infiniteness of God. The religious spirit essentially makes God finite; it reduces him to fit into a man-made box. Or coffin.

Spirit and Truth

Here is a good example in the bible of someone who needed to be freed from this mindset. Below is part of the story of the Samaritan woman whom Jesus met at the well, at the point where she realized she was speaking to a person of authority.

John 4:20-24

Our fathers worshiped in this mountain, and you say that in Jerusalem is the place where men ought to worship. Jesus said to her, Woman, believe Me, the hour is coming when you shall neither worship the Father in this mountain nor yet at Jerusalem. You worship what you do not know, we know what we worship, for salvation is of the Jews. But the hour is coming, and now is, when the true worshipers shall worship the Father in spirit and truth, for the Father seeks such to worship Him. God is a spirit, and they who worship Him must worship in spirit and in truth.

In other words, you've been doing it that way, we've

31

been doing it this way; but in a little while, neither way will matter, because God is not looking on the surface. He's looking at the heart of the worshiper, not his method of worship. Are we worshiping him according to his principles and desires, according to the move of his spirit; or are we making our own patterns more important?

I have walked into unfamiliar settings countless times to work alongside teams with whom I'd never had the opportunity to practice. More often than not, I am asked which songs I plan to do, what songs they should practice, etc, etc. Sometimes I'll have a song or two that I'd like them to look at, but most of the time, I intentionally don't offer any particular "way" I want to perform my portion of the ministry. I do try to ease their minds by telling them that I'm easy to work with, and that I do communicate well. As I mentioned in the first book, it's a skill that is developed over time, and I have a lot of experience using what I've been given to work with in order to convey the message that I hear heaven releasing.

When I begin to lead in these situations, I and the team are already beginning from a place outside of routine.

We have left familiarity and leapt into the depths of the unknown. It can be pretty scary, especially for those who are not accustomed to operating in that level of faith. I, as a leader, am patient, recognizing that we are in this unfamiliar place and that some people might be hesitant to let go of what they know. Do you find yourself nervous about letting go and trusting God in an unfamiliar place of worship? You might be battling a spirit of religion.

An aspect of worshiping in spirit and truth has to do with what God is looking for *in the moment*. This is one way we acknowledge the *person* of God rather than the *concept* of God. A good example is the fact that I love pizza. It's literally my favorite food. Since my wife knows that I love pizza, she used to show her love for me by blessing me with pizza. But here's the thing-- perhaps I didn't want pizza that day; maybe I wanted barbecued ribs (another of my favorites). It has literally made her hesitant over the years to choose a meal for me. She's said that it's too hard to figure me out, and that I'm a complicated man. (Shaft! Raise your hands if you got that joke...) Now, I do look at her heart, and I appreciate the fact that it makes her feel good to bless me; but I told her not to try and figure me out, and to simply ask me what my desire is. God is the same way. With God, it's not just the thought that counts-- it's, "Do you want what I want?" My wife giving me pizza all the time is more blessing the *concept* of James. Her being attuned to my needs and desires is about the *person* of James.

The word "spirit" in Greek and Hebrew means *"breath"* or *"wind"*. It's a movement that cannot simply be captured by our understanding. It is beyond our ways and methods. It moves, as Jesus put it, where it wishes, and no one can pinpoint where it came from or where it's going. The root of the word "truth" in Greek paints a picture of not being concealed. In other words, we must be willing to *be unconcealed,* and just as willing to allow something to be *revealed.* The word says the Spirit leads us into all truth (John 16:13). Because truth is unconcealing and revealing, we will see, do, respond to, and say only what the Lord desires in that moment-- because that is what the spirit does!

Further, (remember, Jesus spoke Aramaic according to history, which is derived from the Hebrew language) the Hebrew word for truth indicates something that is firm, supported, verified to be unshakable. In other words, once the Spirit reveals something, we can bank on its unshakability.

Filled with his desire

Psa 51:15

O Jehovah, open my lips, and my mouth shall show forth Your praise. For You do not desire sacrifice; or else I would give it; You do not delight in burnt offering. The sacrifices of God are a broken spirit; a broken and a contrite heart, O God, You will not despise.

A good way to circumvent a religious atmosphere of worship is to first ask the Lord to fill your mouth. Always begin with the desire to move in that direction, whether you are starting with something familiar or not. Worship in itself is an act of faith, and it must be approached that way if you want to please God. Getting into the routine without looking for the Lord to give you what you need in every situation gives way to a religious spirit.

We also see in the above scripture that the Lord

receives a humble heart that recognizes that it needs him. David was coming from a place of brokenness because of his sin. He knew that the only way he could be justified was by the mercy of God; there was nothing David could offer him except his worship in lowliness and dependence. Jesus explained it another way:

Luke 18:9-14

And He spoke this parable to certain ones who trusted in themselves, that they were righteous, and despised others: Two men went up into the temple to pray; the one a Pharisee, and the other a tax-collector. The Pharisee stood and prayed within himself in this way: God, I thank You that I am not as other men are, extortioners, unjust, adulterers, or even like this tax-collector. I fast twice on the Sabbath, I give tithes of all that I possess. And standing afar off, the tax-collector would not even lift up his eyes to Heaven, but struck on his breast, saying, God be merciful to me a sinner! I tell you, this man went down to his house justified rather than the other. For everyone who exalts himself shall be abased, and he who humbles himself shall be exalted.

This ought to certainly change or challenge the way we

see things. We tend to think we already know what God wants. Many times, our methods are based off of things we feel that we or others have done right or wrong in the past. Then we become so hung up on not doing it a certain way that we develop a religious pattern of not doing it a certain way! I've also heard people say things like, "Yeah, all those old hymns... God ain't doing that anymore. It's time to get on his page." And I've heard others say, "If the worship ain't prophetic, we don't want it." Oh really? Has anyone considered asking God what he is really saying? Do we have the faith to ask him? I've heard leaders sing old hymns, and as far as I could tell, they were moving along EXACTLY the way they should. I've been in atmospheres where people were "trying" to be prophetic, and it felt like a pure disruption to what the Lord was wanting to say or do. We have lifted our efforts above God.

The tax collector in Luke 18 approached the altar with a humble heart. He knew that in order for him to be able to "lift his face", God would have to lift it. *"For everyone who exalts himself shall be abased, and he who humbles himself shall be exalted."* I understand that because many of us are involved in church services or meetings, it's good to have a plan; it's good to be skilled at what you do, etc. If you are a professional trumpet player, break-dancer, opera singer... Great! But we MUST have the mentality that all of this means nothing in his presence; and when we pour out our gift, we are pouring it at his feet, not showcasing our carefully sculpted plans and greatness. In 2 Chronicles 16, it's says that God's eyes are going here and there around the earth, hoping to find those whose hearts are completely turned towards him, so that he can show his power through them.

So I reiterate what I said in the first book-- worshiping him comes first. Worship is not what we are doing, but how we are positioned. The meaning of the word in its original context means to crouch, bow, as to show obeisance. The tax collector took a heart position of bowing before the one who could grant him mercy. Let's stop relegating the concept of worship to church services. As worshipers, we have got to remain in a position of worship without thought to where we are. It's about who he is. It's about what he wants.

A few practical notes

As I've already said a few times, worship is a faith act. We won't know everything all of the time, and we must trust that God is in total control of how he wants to minister his glory, because after all, it's HIS. So some practical steps we can take to assure that we don't fall into the rut of routine are to do things like spontaneously making up a new verse to a song; it's fun and it keeps you, as a leader, on your toes. Take a song that's normally upbeat and make it slow, or vice-versa. Do a song without leading it yourself, and let the congregation lead it. That last one takes its eyes off of the leader and puts it onto our individual and corporate interaction with God. Find your own way to shake things up a bit.

A fault of the modern church is that we have become a very pulpit focused, stage-centric society. Whatever is happening up at the front seems to have more influence in the atmosphere than what God is doing. Here is an excerpt from "Moving With Heaven":

"Many times when I am leading, I see many people waiting for me to do something more than what

39

I am already doing. There is an unnecessary pressure placed on worship leaders to do something more than move in the worship of the one true God. Our purpose is not to "pull something out" of the congregation, although the lord may cause us to declare something as a prophet that serves that purpose. Our purpose is not necessarily to "take" anyone anywhere, although there may be a resident anointing that causes that to happen. (To put it simply, I follow my instruction, then you follow.) The purpose during the time of singing... is to lead in song. As the song leader, singers, and musicians come together, their job is to help foster and facilitate an atmosphere where we can come together and worship, but it's no one's job to cause you to worship. Although Judas Iscariot followed Jesus for three years, his heart was not really with Him. You get what I'm saying? No one can make you worship but you; it's a heart issue..."

A step that I have taken sometimes while doing worship workshops is to literally take the focus off of an individual or stage group by walking around and giving the microphone to random people in the congregation. Now yes, some people are fearful, and others are mic hungry. But the heart of actions like this is to tear the attention away from the "pros" and onto our corporate responsibility to touch God. I've taken many by surprise and done this at big conferences as well. You'll find it's more freeing for you and everyone else to make God the real focus. I had one particular Korean church express to me that their worship gatherings have never been the same to this day, since we shifted the focus from the pulpit and onto everyone connecting with the Lord. A boldness and passion have risen in them to worship and interact with the person of God.

Keep it simple. If there is one thing I've found that a spirit of legalism and religion continually and successfully perpetrates, it's to make things complicated. But in actuality, it's the simple things that seem to have the most impact, as God uses the foolish things of this world to display his power. Be intentional about not complicating things. And know that you won't need to understand everything. Trying hard to understand also complicates things; just move the way you see God moving. I know a Nigerian worship leader who simply uses vowel chants-- his chants take up more than half of some of his songs! Oh, but it's glorious, and connects us to the simplicity of reaching God, and also personalizes our communication with him. I've sung "Holy, holy, holy" over and over, knowing that there were squirming spirits in the room, wishing I'd move on and sing something "deeper." But God *is* deep! Not *complicated*; deep.

Also, don't become stuck in one particular way of doing things. An example is creating the sound of warfare. When we think "warfare", most of us automatically think of booming drums, shouting voices, swinging flags and swords, etc. An example I use when discussing this subject is that in Judges 4, the battle was essentially decided in the quietness of Jael's tent! Be sensitive to the movement of heaven in the moment; heaven is beyond our methods. The word "holy", that I mentioned above, is an all-encompassing word that seems to sum up everything we aren't able to put into words about God. It is a powerful tool in warfare, even when there are no explosive sounds coming from the music. Again, if we make it about our way, we neglect the potential for God's power and glory to manifest; but if we make it about him, the enemy must bow. Demons respond to authority and power, not loud sounds and swinging swords. All of those things are good. Sometimes it should be clamorous and fierce, and the symbolism can be faith-lifting-- especially if it's what

God is doing. But the key is to *move with God.*

As a final thought, don't be afraid to *do* or *be* new in the midst of a religious atmosphere. If you'll look at it like a war, you'll see that this religious spirit is attempting to keep you within its grip, operating under its principles. Perhaps you are part of a ministry that only allows you to worship in a particular way. "Sneak" the new into the course of your leading. Have the drums do a solo or something. Lead the congregation in a series of chants or shouts, maybe causing them to repeat what God is saying. Then go back to they way they do things. The more I've done these things in certain places I've ministered, the more I'm trusted to lead however I see fit; they can see that God is in the midst of what I'm doing. On the other hand, you can't be afraid to be ridiculed or disliked because of your freedom to worship and your heart to please God. I'd rather be kicked out of church than have to fully submit to a restrictive, filthy, religious spirit. The Lord is worth it.

Stay free.

IV. The Real Tabernacle of Worship

Amos 9:11-12 (NKJV)

"On that day I will raise up The tabernacle of David, which has fallen down, and repair its damages; I will raise up its ruins, and rebuild it as in the days of old; That they may possess the remnant of Edom, and all the Gentiles who are called by My name," says the Lord who does this thing.

The Lord says that he is restoring David's tabernacle. After all is done, there will be no need for a preacher, prophet, etc, because he will dwell among us (Rev. 21:3). But what we are doing-- celebrating and ministering to the Lord, being near him and knowing him more and more-- that will last forever.

God has a desire. It's a desire that goes beyond the function of a church or ministry. In the last book I mentioned studying the teachings of Jesus. They are very pertinent to learning about the true heart of God toward his people and purposes. If you remember,

Jesus spent some time in the synagogues, but most of his time was spent among the people. While the gathering in the synagogue was a vital aspect of worship, Jesus said that "those who are well have no need of a physician, but those who are sick" (Luke 5:27-32). What does this mean for us?

As worshipers and leaders, we tend to relate what we do solely to a church service or some sort of Christian gathering where we all come together, sing, dance, raise our hands, etc. It's very important to do those things, but as those with the heart and voice of God, it seems that until now, we haven't realized the power of what we do. The lord said in Amos 9 that the tabernacle of David would be raised in the midst of all the judgment on the wicked, perverse kingdoms. As a result, the nations he has called would be possessed and covered by what he is building. Your act of worship to God should extend beyond the four walls of the church setting, in heart *and* in action. If you are the head of a ministry, church, apostolic center, etc., your mission should somehow point outside of the confines of what we know as church today. Who or what is being affected? How are things moving or changing as a result of what you are doing?

I remember being so frustrated because I felt like all I was doing was singing at people from a stage. Although experiences with God were very real in those times, it felt to me like praise and worship leading was all about church. However, it wasn't a location issue; it turned out to be a heart issue. Remember, worship is a position more than an action, according to the Hebrew meaning of the word. How is my heart positioned as I am performing my service before God? I decided to change my position by asking the Lord to show me what he is looking for from me, and having my heart fully vested in following that through.

I then had to decide that I'd physically change my position as well. Knowing that we are living vessels of God, carrying his spirit wherever we are, I had to decide that I'd be open to hearing him and then responding wherever I was. As a song leader, I began to sing the purpose of God into whatever atmosphere I was in, whether it be a grocery store, at the park, at a church conference, restaurant, etc. I even began hearing the lord direct me to take special trips and assignments to go and release a sound in particular places-- *outside of gatherings*-- so I responded by faith to go and do just as he said. God is not only concerned about the mission of running a ministry. He cares about the purpose for which he created us-- to glorify him, to steward what he's given us, and multiply it. In multiplying we actually *do* glorify him; and just as the Lord placed Adam in the garden to guard and steward it, we should be doing the same thing with whatever he has given us.

If you read 1 Chronicles chapters 25-27, you'll find that David's system of worship began with those who ministered to the lord through sound. This sound continued night and day. They prophesied (by inspiration, and given authority to prophesy by David (1 Chr 25:2)), praised, played instruments, etc. But it didn't stop there. Typically, when we mention David's Tabernacle, we think continual praise and worship. If you read on, you'll find that it went from there out to other duties, like groundskeeping, treasury, etc. Then it went even further out, into daily business, like vineyards and wine cellars and other things. So it doesn't end with sound and prophesy-- it *begins* with it.

When the ark returned to Israel in 2 Samuel, David's full attention and desire was given to establishing the presence of God over his nation. The worship of God had preeminence over everything else. He knew that as king of Israel, he'd been given stewardship of God's presence in that nation. He set up a tabernacle for the ark-- a *tent*-- and put everyone in place to minister before God. It wasn't about anything or anyone else accept being where God was (Psalm 84), and God's place as true king and lord over Israel. These are the things we must keep in mind when we speak of David's tabernacle. Our goal as a worshiper should be to lift God high above everything else, and to establish an altar of worship where we stand. What we don't seem to understand is that our heart and intentions are directly related to how the altar is being built. Saul's altar of sacrifice was rejected by God (1 Samuel 13, 1 Samuel 15). I believe one of the major reasons was because Saul didn't truly care at all about the presence of God; he cared about himself and his own kingdom. Yet David, who broke so many Levitical laws of worship and committed heinous acts that rivaled Saul's, God called a "man after my own heart" (1 Samuel 13:14, Acts 13:22). David had a pure heart of worship towards God, with no hidden or selfish agendas when it came to building an altar of worship.

It's easy to fall into what I'm calling the "Saul rut" when we don't have a pure heart towards God. Allow me to "bring it home" a bit for some of us. Do you find yourself caring about perfection more than glorifying God? Does *relevance* drive you more than God's *presence*? (No matter what anyone tells you, the two are in no way related.) Do your worries keep your focus on yourself instead of who God is and what he wants to do? Do things in your atmosphere (religious activities, circumstances, etc.) diminish the reality of God as a person, causing you to relate more to him as a *thing* or *something to do*? We will never establish a pure altar of worship if we don't address the issues that keep us in the Saul rut. I make a practice of submitting my heart and intentions to the Lord, especially when I endeavor to lift him up before men. I address any issues of pride and insincerity, impurity, and whatever else can trap me in a selfish mindset. Don't think of this as a method; look at it as a heart attitude. In other words, you don't have to repeat the prayer, but like David, continue to get real with God, and not let the world revolve around you and how you perceive things.

At the heart of David's tabernacle was the concept of God's presence dwelling among men. It's a breaking out of the curse of Adam (whose sin separated men from God) and into the eternal intent of Yahweh. David's faith to build a tabernacle that was not done according to Mosaic law (where only the high priest could minister before the ark under strict customs and laws that bore the penalty of death) was a giant leap into eternity. The Messiah had not even come yet, and would not for over 1,000 years; yet David *stepped into* a ripping of the veil that separated God from men. He stepped into eternal purpose.

Rev 21:3 *And I heard a great voice out of Heaven saying, Behold, the tabernacle of God is with men, and He will dwell with them, and they will be His people, and God Himself will be with them and be their God.*

David's tabernacle was a picture of the future that God has for his people. When we step into a place to change the atmosphere, we must endeavor to connect to each other within God's eternal purpose. How does he see it? What is his vision? Do we hear or sense what he is saying about it? The "four walls" mindset of worship will keep us from realizing God's full plan, because we allow our senses to be limited by that mentality and its concerns. Even paralyzing divisions take place because of this, halting the work of heaven and placing chains of iniquity on what was meant to be mobilized in faith, hope, and love. It's a bondage he never intended for us; it's a prison of fleshly works that have no place in eternity:

Mat 7:21-23 *Not everyone who says to Me, Lord! Lord! shall enter the kingdom of Heaven, but he who does the will of My Father in Heaven. Many will say to Me in that day, Lord! Lord! Did we not prophesy in Your name, and through Your name throw out demons, and through Your name do many wonderful works? And then I will say to them I never knew you! Depart from Me, those working lawlessness!*

Just like the results of falling into the "Saul rut", the lord counts everything we do "in his name" that was not his will, as lawlessness. Be careful not to fashion yourself, as a worshiper, after temporary things. The Lord says that heaven and earth will pass away, but his words will always remain. And remember, he didn't say *"the bible"*-- he said his *"words"* will not pass away (Mat 24:35). Everything that he has declared and desired, we endeavor to surround ourselves with and fashion ourselves through. We desire to love the Lord in such a way that we are willing to break protocol for the sake of *his* purpose, not our own.

So everywhere we place our feet has the potential to become a pure altar of worship to the Lord, because he dwells with us and we with him. We can "activate" eternal purpose wherever we are if we disconnect from legalism, nonproductive religious activities, and selfish gain; and connect to God's true desire.

The best picture I can think of when it comes to David's tabernacle is this: Heaven to Earth. In the book of Isaiah, in Revelation, the Lord speaks of the Key of David (more on this later). This key gave the ability to lock and unlock doors that no man could control or counteract. With the Key of David, we are able to access a place of glory in God that opens that realm to wherever we are on earth. I believe David accessed this "key" not simply because he was favored to have it, but because he recognized that God was beyond the law; God was beyond the rituals of worship. David believed that he could know God *beyond*. So he established a way of worship that represented heaven on earth. And God was apparently so moved by David's faith and heart towards him that he established David forever.

Again, when we approach God, we approach from the eternal place. Worshiping with the faith that we are right in the midst of heaven-- though our feet are on this earthly ground-- displays the same faith that David had. Every access that this key gave David is available to us. Sometimes we must simply desire and envision that there is no barrier between us and God, then move as though that is the case. When Jesus gave himself as a sacrifice, the veil of the temple (that separated laymen and even most clergy from the Holy of Holies) tore in two, didn't it? When I worship, I know that I am standing before God, because Jesus' blood gave me access to go places that I could not go without it. Don't believe anyone who tries to give you more "keys" than this to enter in to God's presence. His word says that he is with us always; and if he is the door, and his blood makes us acceptable, heaven has come to earth right where we stand. Fullness of glory is available right there. Salvation. Healing. Miracles. Revelation. Fullness.

God, here we are; it's not about our own works and temporary things that will pass away. Let your tabernacle cover the nations and draw many to the glory of your covering.

All the things we prophesy will eventually fade away

Knowledge that we've gained,

Skills that we've attained will all wither away

I endeavor to love you.

~excerpt from the song, "My Endeavor" by James Vincent and Bethany Martin

V. Back to Communion

The lord is continually calling our attention back to communion; his desire is for us to dwell with him in the secret place. What does that mean? Don't we worship every Sunday? sometimes more? We try to put him first, we pray, we do what we know to do according to his word... What does he mean?

The lord gave me two dreams that I'd like to share. Although I won't go in depth as to what every detail means, I will share them in their entirety. Both of these dreams paint deep, specific pictures that I hope can help us.

In the first dream, there was a lot going on in a huge mall-like building. There were people going here and there, very busy. I knew that all of the busyness that was occurring had to do with a christian conference that was happening there. I'm not sure to what capacity I was involved, but I had some important part to play in this conference. There was a line outside of the meeting room for people who were purchasing items (not sure what) that stretched into the room. I walked to the front of the room to the front row of seats and sat down. Two men walked up to me; one I knew, and the introduced himself. We shook hands. He knew me apparently, but I didn't know him. He was wearing my blue shirt, so I said, "Oh, I see he's got you wearing my shirt, huh?" We laughed, and I went back to whatever I was doing. The line of people had been moved by then since the meeting was beginning again; we were on some sort of break.

I knew I had to get upstairs to change clothes, so I started to get up. At that time, a young African lady sat at the piano and began to play. There was such a glorious sound coming from that girl that I couldn't move. I sat down and "soaked" in the sounds that were coming forth. It had gotten to the point that I would simply think a sound, then she'd play it. It was incredible.

Some of you are called to lead ministries. Some are called to train people. Some are called to one thing and others to another, but if we become so caught up in the function and busyness and chaos of things that we lose that intimate place of worship; that part of us that always responds to his voice... we are in the wrong place-- there are no two ways about it. Don't you know that you can be doing what you think is the will of God, believe you're serving him whole-heartedly, and be rejected by him? (Matthew 7:21-23)

What is it that he wants? (2 Chr 15&16) 2 Chronicles 15:2 says, "The lord is with you, while you are with him, and **if you seek him**, he will be found by you. But **if you forsake him,** he will forsake you." To seek him is to find him, to find him is to know him, because when you find him, he reveals himself. It's all over the word of God.

Jesus defined the object of our seeking in Matt 6:33: "Seek first the kingdom of God, and His righteousness, and all these things will be added to you."

Where are your desires placed? There are many things I want. I like things. I like food. I like my wife to do certain things. I like my kids to behave a certain way. I like to look good. I like to do good. I like things to run smoothly. Really. I called my wife once, reveling in the fact that everything went correctly all day… that's a big deal to me. But I also clearly remember a conversation I had with my wife a couple of years ago, where I expressed my heart to her in tears: "I have done many things, good and bad. I've been blessed, been many places. But at the heart of everything, I just want to be where He is." In the words of singer Alicia Keys, *"Everything means nothing"* if I don't have him.

2Chr 16:9 says, "For the eyes of the lord run to and fro throughout the whole earth, to show himself strong on behalf of them whose heart is **perfect** toward him… In this you have done foolishly..." This word, "perfect" is "**shalem,**" where we get the word "shalom." It means "*whole* or *complete.*" So the lord desires to show himself mighty on behalf of those whose hearts are *wholly and completely* toward him.

Intimacy and communion with God have carried a sort of stigma with it, of mushiness and sappiness. In actuality, not only is it a place of love, it is a place of incredible glory, power, and might. One who is wholly dedicated to seeking him will, without a doubt, find him, and have a door of his glory opened to him. The mightiest warriors in the bible were people who were not simply people of God, but people who were close to God (Joshua, David). I recently prayed this prayer: *Lord, I don't want to be "well versed", I want to be one with you.*

In the dream, I had things to do, things to accomplish, I was important. But my heart was so with the lord that when he called to me through the African girl playing the piano, I couldn't help but respond. Suddenly everything else became unimportant. I was reminded that my time was his time. Everything stopped for me. He had free reign in my life, and even my very thoughts were right in time and tune with his.

I have this little thing that I do with my youngest son. One of my nicknames for him is "That Daddy Boy." No matter what he is doing, playing, watching TV, bathing; if I call out, "That--" he finishes, "Daddy Boy!" My call cuts through every part of him and causes him to respond, no matter what. Now, there are times that he will intentionally not answer; though he hears the call, he hides behind a door and makes a game out of it. Are we playing that game with the

Lord? Think on that.

Religion vs. Communion

The lord once defined the spirit of religion for me, as we talked about earlier. The bible defines what religion is supposed to be, but we kind of throw that word around and it carries a bad connotation for us. But religion in and of itself is not a bad thing. We say, "that's so religious," or, "don't be religious" every time something of a legalistic or methodical nature rises up, or even when our level in our walk with God is challenged. Selah. But this is what the lord told me:

Being guilty of a spirit of religion is when you and your ways and standards become bigger than God. The spirit of religion opposes the spirit of communion. It literally keeps us out of his presence. His word says so-- he detests it.

Looking good, sounding good, being good are not bad things. They're great. The lord has given us these things. Even worshiping a certain way isn't bad. But are you willing to lay it all down for what actually pleases him? Are you willing to be moved at the sound of his voice? Are you willing to *STOP and hear him?* Examine yourself: do your desires take second place to the will of God? Are you willing to change your way of doing things for his purpose? And-- a*re you willing to allow the seeking to take precedence over what you think you already know or have attained? As soon as you stop seeking him, you have fallen prey to a spirit of religion; you've fallen prey to the object of God's detestation.* A "heart perfect towards him" desires only to please him. The fact that Asa sought out the king of Syria spoke to the fact that his heart was perfect only towards himself. Even when the prophet corrected him about it, Asa despised him so much that he threw him in prison! Here's the thing-- Asa WON that war. His plan WORKED. But it was not the will of the lord for him to do it the way he did it. **Don't forget about all the wonderful things the people said they did, right before the lord declared, "I never knew you..."**

The event that sealed Saul's fate was the fact that he sought a witch instead of God. Remember 1Chr 14 (read it if you're not familiar with it)-- "Shall I go up?" David sought the lord both times in that passage, and he gave him different answers for the same type of situation, each time attaining the victory God had

61

planned for him.

The Key of David

Is 22:20-23 (KJV) And *it shall come to pass in that day, that I will call **my servant Eliakim** the son of Hilkiah:_And I will clothe him with thy robe, and strengthen him with thy girdle, and I will commit thy government into his hand: and he shall be a father to the inhabitants of Jerusalem, and to the house of Judah._And the key of the house of David will I lay upon his shoulder; so he shall open, and none shall shut; and he shall shut, and none shall open._And I will fasten him as a nail in a sure place; and he shall be for a glorious throne to his father's house.*

Who was Eliakim? He was the official appointed over the entire household of the king. He carried out the king's request. In the king's absence, he was the "head honcho," if you will. He had authority to freely address the king, the ability to interact within the king's affairs with the authority of the king himself. It is interesting that the lord in the book of Isaiah said that he (Eliakim), not Hezekiah (who was king at the time), would be given the key of David. I believe King Hezekiah could be seen here as a picture of God the father. Eliakim was intimate with the king and his house. He knew everything. He was close to the king. Everything that had to do with the household of the king had to go through the one who was head of household.

So here, it serves to say that David had a revelation. There was an intimacy with God that allowed him access to any and every door, as there is nothing that does not originally belong to God. There was an intimacy with God that caused David to see the revelation the lord was pouring out over the land. David prophesied because of these revelations. His heart was so turned towards the lord that he wouldn't do anything without knowing whether or not it would please the lord. Yes, he messed up quite a bit-- but the lord himself declared David a "man after my own heart." This key that David possessed allowed him access to more than just a seat upon a throne. He was near to God's heart.

This intimacy with God started in the field, when he was just a shepherd, before anyone ever knew who he was. He worshiped and learned about God's ways in that intimate place. When he left that job and took on the job of fighting Goliath, it was from that place of worship that he had the confidence to take him down. (1Sam 17:26, 45-47) He then moved on to being a captain over Saul's army. Then he married into the king's family. Throughout all of Saul's antics and attempts to either kill or have him killed, the word says continually of David, "*...the lord was with him.*"

Read the Psalms. Many of them were written by David himself, and whether he was rejoicing, sorrowful, prayerful, afraid, prophesying... he was communing with the lord. These psalms were written at many different points in David's life. They are evidence of his close relationship with the Lord. His heart remained in that place of seeking-- that place of intimacy and awareness of God-- from the time he was herding sheep up until his last days as king of all Israel.

David's relationship with God was unique. Many of the things David did were unorthodox; things that would be considered violations against Mosaic law. But he had a different door of access. He held a "key" that allowed him access to places that others could not go because of his relationship with the Father. This key gave him authority in unusual places, access to doors that could not naturally be opened or shut by just anyone.

So I believe that Eliakim in Isaiah 22 not only represents a type of Christ, but also represents what the lord desires to do in us. Remember, Christ is our forerunner (Heb 6:20). The Key of David opens up all that David was, had, and had access to. And the lord promised that David's kingdom would last forever! It is available today for all who are in Jesus.

The lord is offering us at this time an open door. This door was referenced in Rev 3:7-13, when he told the church at Philadelphia that an open door was set before them. Through this door is a place of solidarity, steadfastness, and confidence through Jesus Christ. Through this door is promotion to a place of glory in God. (That's what happened with Eliakim, that's what happened with the church in Philadelphia.)

The key of David opened the holy of holies when Jesus was on the cross... It's done. We already have direct access.

This takes me to my second dream:

I was standing beside a huge platform watching another worship leader lead worship. I remember saying to myself, "Wow, this guy has an awesome voice." But I couldn't help wondering if he really knew how to connect with heaven. I then left and went to the back where there were a group of soldiers. These were all worshipers dressed in military uniform. I held some kind of rank, like a high ranking low rank, if that makes any sense. I held a great deal of authority where I was, and although I wasn't the highest rank, I was the strongest/most skilled. I was also in uniform. It was my job to teach them to honor the higher ranking officials, to raise them up in God's army. We were preparing to fight some sort of evil that was expected to enter the atmosphere. I stepped out of the line of officers I was in and began to bark at the privates, yelling, "Are you asleep soldier? Are you asleep, soldier?"

Just then, an officer who ranked higher than I came and grabbed me by the arm. He led me up to a platform, like a stage, where there were people, almost in a daze, looking out through double doors. There were open umbrellas, such that people use for filming

66

or photography blocking the doorway. I thought that the officer wanted me to use my connection with heaven to combat something since I had that ability. So I asked, "What is all this?"

The officer said, "Just listen." At that moment, I heard a most beautiful sound. There was a heavenly male-like voice singing, "Holy, Holy…" We knew it was non-earthly. People looked and listened in awe, but I couldn't. I bowed to the ground and began to weep uncontrollably.

I initially thought I was being summoned for one thing, but the Lord simply wanted me to listen. What I heard caused me to fall to my knees. I had become so caught up in my function and assignment that:

1. I didn't see the door that was open
2. I couldn't immediately hear the sound that was coming from heaven.

And that sound was a deep place of worship, a sound straight from the throne. It was the sound beckoning me to that "better part" spoken of by Jesus about

Martha's sister, Mary (Luke 10:38-42).

It is important to note that the lord knows that "holy, holy, holy" (as was being sung in the dream) is something that draws me straight into his glory... It plays the strings of my heart; it's my connection in him.

Stop. Pull away (as Jesus did). Wait. Listen. the lord, who holds the key of David, has opened a door before us. Come and commune, dine at his table with him. Come know him again. Hear what he's saying to you NOW. Sit and relax with him. It's ok to *not* have a plan or objective. Just be with him. WE MUST be willing to drop everything in order to follow and be where he is. Revelation, strategies, answers, miracles, healing, all his glory opens up to us from that place--- but HE must be number one.

Amen.

VI. Praise

I have included this brief study on praise in order to help us see how much we have limited ourselves in the area of relating to the person of God. The title of this chapter is a bit deceptive, however. Although I intend to sort of break down the Hebrew words that we typically translate and associate with praise, I want to broaden our perspective on the actual pictures these words represent.

When I read God's word, I always ask him to show me the fullness of what he is saying. I know the bible has been translated and rewritten so many times that certain pictures and concepts get lost, depth becomes watered down, and some things are even shaped according to man's conditional understanding rather than what was originally being conveyed. Word studies are helpful. Knowing God is even more helpful. So I ask him to open up the scriptures to me, much like Jesus did on the road to Emmaus.

I mentioned in the previous chapter that in Matthew 24, Jesus says that even if heaven and earth pass away, his words would never pass away. The word used in the Greek there is *logos*, which means word, as in something *said,* not simply written. When we read the logos, we must recognize that we are reading a record of something that actually happened or was actually spoken forth. What gives the word it's power is recognizing that it is alive. "Logos" is a sound that is alive and full of motion, as opposed to something printed with ink. As we look at the words that we normally translate as "praise", let's discover what was actually spoken forth. I believe this quick study will help those who consider themselves bible scholars as well!

HEBREW WORDS FOR PRAISE

To understand the original "logos", let's first erase the word "praise" from our brain for a moment. Understand that the English word "praise" is used many times in the Old Testament for several different words that have very different meanings. Imagine a speaker of the original language saying the actual Hebrew words that I am about to show you, instead of thinking "praise". You'll find that most of the time, the speaker was painting a deeper picture than we may have realized, and that many times, the actual meaning of the words used can shift with the context.

YADAH: Stretching forth of hands is the picture given here. It's like an extension of what is stirring on the inside-- thanksgiving, praise, joy, etc. Stretching forth of hands is representative of the extension of self, in acknowledgment of what you are extending yourself towards.

The first time it is used in in Genesis 29:35, when Leah bore Judah. After Jacob wed Leah, Laban gave him a week with her, then gave him Rachel, whom he really loved. Jacob chose to share a home with Rachel. Leah felt unloved, and with every child she bore, she thought Jacob would finally choose to share a home with her.

In verse 35, this was now her fourth child, and now she chose to extend herself to and acknowledge the Lord because he continued to bless her womb.

Gen 29:35 *And she conceived again, and bore a son; and she said, This time I will **praise** Jehovah. Therefore* *she called his name Judah, and quit bearing.*

Some translations say, "'*Now*' I will praise the Lord..." That word, "*now*", is actually a sequential word, as in a rhythm. The King James Version is most accurate by saying "*This time...*". As we read on in the following chapter and verses, it becomes apparent that she had finally accepted her position in Jacob's life, and decided to take the position of keeping her hand outstretched to the Lord. So in the context of what we know about Leah, here is what we read:

This time (as opposed to the three previous times, where her hope was in Jacob) *I YADAH the Lord... And named her child Judah* (her reason to *yadah*, or stretch her hands forth).

Judah is mostly associated with being the praise and war tribe, which is true; but according to what we've just learned, it's more the embodiment of *purpose* or *reasons* to praise, celebrate, war with, or extend to the Lord. It's about what is actually *in* one's hand, so to speak. So when we think "Judah" and/or "yadah", let's think of what it means within the context of the moment. David (who fittingly was of the tribe of Judah) was a prime example in 1Samuel 17, when he heard the

Philistine giant cursing Israel, and was moved to extend himself to enter the war and glorify God by killing him.

TODAH: The word used in Hebrew for thanks; it's like acknowledgment, as in rank, deeds, status, agreement, etc. One of the definitions for "thank" is "to hold responsible, or attribute". It isn't solely linked to gratitude. It's also linked to *yadah;* an extension of the hand, as a handshake or agreement. Let's look at Ps 42:2-5.

Psa 42:2-5

*My soul thirsts for God, for the living God; when shall I come and appear before God? My tears have been my food day and night, while they say to me all the day, Where is your God? When I remember these things, I pour out my soul on me; for I had gone with the multitude; I went with them to the house of God with the voice of joy and **praise**, a multitude keeping the feast. Why are you cast down, O my soul, and moan within me? Hope in God; for I shall **praise** Him for the salvation of His face.*

Reading this scripture in many of our own languages,

we'd never know that the two words used here are not exactly the same. We'd be thinking "praise" in the context of saying good things about the Lord, singing songs of praise and worship, etc. The word in verse 4 is actually "todah", while the word in verse 5 is "yadah". Let's read it differently now.

Ps 42:4 I went with them to the house of God with *shouts* and *todah*... again, it's important to associate words like yadah and todah with the context. In this verse, it appears the author is reflecting on a joyous time, so it was with shouting and *thanksgiving,* or *acknowledgment* towards the Lord that he went to the house of God. "Praise" doesn't give the most accurate picture here; it somewhat limits what is really being expressed.

Ps 42:5 I shall yet *yadah* him for the help of his countenance (KJV). **I am continually stretched forth to him; my hands are ever extended to him for the salvation of his countenance.** The word "praise" is quite inaccurate here as well.

Ps 42:11 Why are you cast down, O my soul? And why are you disquieted within me? Hope in God, for I shall yet YADAH him, the savior of my countenance, and my

God. **In other words, don't be so filled with despair, soul! You have a Savior to extend yourself to, who will lift your face.**

SHABACH: A loud sound that causes everything around to recognize and come into alignment with its definitiveness. The spirit behind this word is an "irrefutability"... it's a victorious, powerful sound. It can be a (loud) statement that brings everything into subjection to it.

Psa 145:4 *One generation shall praise Your works to another, and shall declare Your mighty acts.*

A more precise translation would be:

Ps. 145:4 Generation to generation will *"**shabach** the memory of"* your wondrous works, and shall declare your mighty acts.

Because of the power of this sound, I believe generations can be saved and brought into alignment with the purpose of God if we would open our mouths and continually shabach into the atmosphere; and not only the atmosphere, but in the hearing of our children as well.

Sometimes, the fact that I use a shabach sound even in "sweet" situations somehow causes whatever I'm singing to be definite. I have sung, "He looooooooves you..." and someone suddenly believed it, and it was like something broke off of them.

When David faced Goliath, he began to shabach against the curses that were being declared over Israel:

1Sa 17:43-47 *And the Philistine said to David, Am I a dog that you come to me with sticks? And the Philistine cursed David by his gods. And the Philistine said to David, Come to me, and I will give your flesh to the birds of the air and to the beasts of the field. And David said to the Philistine, You come to me with a sword and with a spear and with a javelin. But I come to you in the name of Jehovah of Hosts, the God of the armies of Israel, whom you have defied. Jehovah will deliver you into my hand today, and I will strike you and take your head from you and give the bodies of the army of the Philistines to the birds of the air today, and to the wild beasts of the earth, so that all the earth may know that there is a God in Israel. And all this multitude shall know that Jehovah does not save with sword and spear; for the battle is Jehovah's, and He will give you into our hands.*

Then the Lord backed up his bold declaration!

BARAK: It's actually a posture, physically and figuratively. It means to *bow the knee*, in honor and blessing. When Rachel wasn't bearing any children for Jacob, she gave Jacob her maid Bilhah (read Genesis 30), saying, "that she might bear upon my *knees*." Basically, that Bilhah would be doing all the work, but Rachel's house would be blessed because of it... Bilhah is standing in for Rachel in order to bring blessing.

What does this mean? It brings a whole new picture to what it means to bless and be blessed. When you bless, it's like gaining access to favor. "He who exalts himself will be humbled, but he who humbles himself will be exalted." (Luke 14:11) So when we sing, "I will BLESS the Lord..." Understand that there is like an homage being paid to one who is greater, (like Abraham and Melchizedek in Genesis 14) and then there is something being poured back onto you as you address him in humility.

In the Hebrew way of thinking (since this was originally written in Hebrew), there is not one thing that happens without affecting another. Even in philosophy and science, they say for every action, there is an opposite reaction. So if you are honoring someone else, you are in effect humbling yourself. For our own heart's sake, that's the way we need to look at it.

Bilhah became fruitful as she took the position of blessing Jacob's house by becoming his wife in honor of Rachel.

Many of us read Genesis 14 and see where Abraham gave Melchizedek a tenth of all he had, and see that as "blessing". In actuality, it was more like *"todah"*, acknowledging the gift and position of Melchizedek. But before that, something magnificent happens. The word says that Melchizedek, king of Salem and high priest of the Most High God, met Abraham with bread and wine, and "blessed" him. We typically look at the prayer he prayed and simply think that was the blessing, when in actuality, the word is "barak", which we learned means "to bow the knee." Now, whether he physically knelt, I suppose we wouldn't know; but a *position* of humility is being portrayed as he honored Abraham. Think about that-- how even God himself told Abraham that he would *barak* those who *barak* him (Genesis 12). There is such weightiness in the notion that God, the possessor of heaven and earth, would honor us in that way. So powerful.

HALLEL: to be clear, to shine, to boast, show, to rave, celebrate, to be clamorously foolish... It's the most clear word used to define what we know as our English word, "praise." When David declares, "Praise the Lord (Hallelujah)", it is a command to boast, show, rave, celebrate, be clamorously foolish! Then he lists reasons to celebrate!

ZAMAR: Strike strings, making music... An artful, skillful expression; Using your being to make music, to create through skill; it's a picture of using your fingers skillfully, as in playing a harp.

This is one of my two favorite words on the list. It brings me great joy to be able to use my gift of creating music to glorify God.

It's the exact same word used when the Lord speaks about pruning the vineyard in Leviticus 25... For six years, you can **zamar** the vineyard. The seventh year, don't zamar. In other words, don't carry out the duties of skillfully caring for the vineyard in the seventh year;

don't **orchestrate** the duties of the vineyard that year.

You have to see, you must anticipate, you must be counteractive, adjustable, and knowledgeable. A better way to put that-- so that no one will deem themselves unqualified-- is to be *intentional.* Be intentional about the sound you make before the Lord. It doesn't only include music; not at the heart of the word. Be skillful in your worship. An example would be found in Colossians 3:23-24: "...whatever your hand finds to do, do it with all your might..."

Another interesting tidbit is the fact that the name of the mountain goat, *chamois* (Deut 14:5), comes from the same root as zamar. The chamois is very light on its feet, and like other mountain goats, it is very skilled at navigating through rocky terrain even when it is being pursued by predators.

TEHILLAH: A song of laud.

Is there any need to tell you why this is my other favorite word that's associated with praise? I don't think I need to give an in-depth dissertation on the meaning of this word-- it's straight forward. It's essentially the song version of *"hallel."*

Notice that it is a *celebratory* song of praise. It's also a song that displays the fact that the object of the song is worth the worshiper looking and sounding clamorously foolish! Whether the song is an upbeat or slower tempo, its focus is to celebrate or boast with the intention of bringing all attention to whatever it is we are celebrating, raving, or boasting about.

Let's take a look at this scripture that uses four of the words in one verse. Knowing what's actually being said here brings it to life!

Psa 100:3 *Know that Jehovah, He is God. He has made us, and not we ourselves; we are His people, and the sheep of his pasture.*

Psa 100:4 *Enter into His gates with thanksgiving, into His courts with praise; be thankful to Him, bless His name.*

And now, verse 4 with what we've discussed:

Ps 100:4 Enter into his gates with thanksgiving **((todah) reference to verse 3)**, into his courts with

81

praise **((tehillah)with songs of laud)**: be thankful **((yadah) stretch out your hands, extend your being)** unto him, and bless **((barak)bow the knee in honor before)** his name.

And then you'll see that towards you:

Ps 100:5 *For the Lord is good, his mercy everlasting, and his truth to all generations.*

Hallelujah!!!

I love this study, because it brings to life all of the different aspects of releasing to and from God. I don't look at this list as words for "praise", I look at this list as expanding our horizon of release and relation to him. As a matter of fact, I believe more words from the bible can be added to this list, since we've established that not all of these words necessarily mean "praise" in their own context!

Ask the Lord to speak clearly to you when you seek to learn him through his word; it will become something very supernatural that invariably leaks into your moving with him in your release of worship. It will also force you to address some of the religious type of mindsets that have formed over years of having the word interpreted through a limited view of who God truly is. Certain dance movements will be less viewed as sensual and worldly as we see how God sees. Certain sounds will be heard through heavenly ears, and not simply through how we've been legalistically programmed to hear them as we allow God to broaden our heavenly senses and our understanding of his true words. Remember, we don't simply *interpret* God-- he *reveals* to us. By his spirit, we discern good and evil.

He speaks *beyond*; and we don't have to do much more than a few "logos" studies to see how much we truly don't know!

VII. Apostolic Worship

I need to begin by saying that over these past few decades, we have seen and heard a whole lot about apostles, where it seems that concept had been silent for a several hundred years. The modern church, for the longest time, has been very resistant to this concept. I have had arguments with minister friends over this very thing. It is a divisive subject. I will say, however, that whatever label we decide to give something doesn't change what that thing really is. I personally believe that there have *always* been apostles operating in this world since the last of the original twelve died. We've just had an aversion to calling it what it is.

Understand-- to reject any gift of God is *to reject God*. The word tells us that the ministry of the likes of apostles, prophets, pastors, teachers, evangelists, are gifts that the lord gave to equip the body. (Ephesians 4:9-12) When we refuse to accept what he has given for our benefit, we are refusing to receive all that God is. We can not-- make no mistake about it-- become or fulfill all that God has created us to be and do when we don't believe in all that he is. Hear me worshipers, you are more than what you think you are. You are more than a good singer or dancer. You are more than a great pianist! Receive the fullness of God and enter a glorious world of discovering all that he will do through your gift.

That said, many have asked me, "What is the difference between *prophetic* worship and *apostolic* worship?" I become a bit hesitant to answer this, because I am fully aware that people can form a doctrine or mindset around certain definitions. I normally tell people that I don't differentiate the two; worship to God is something that must be done in spirit and truth, regardless of how we want to label it. I personally feel that worship is too sacred to try to break it down to something we can "handle" as mere men.

I do, however, understand that there is a movement happening in the earth that is unlike previous seasons, at least on a grander scale. As many begin to come to the understanding of what it means to be "sent out", there is a culture of people who desire to see the kingdom of God influence more than just their churches and homes. Just as an apostle, by definition, is one who is sent out for the purpose of reforming or influencing a particular sphere in the name of the one who sent him or her, there are worshipers who are hearing the call of God to move into spheres beyond their typically accepted role. The key word when speaking of the apostolic is *"sent"*.

Being an apostle DOES NOT NECESSARILY MEAN being in charge; in fact, he or she has no authority at all unless he is *sent*. (The "title" of Apostle literally means nothing at all in God.) Then, there is the purpose for which he is sent. So an apostolic worshiper is one who can be sent to influence and establish the purpose of God through sound, whatever arena that might be. This is an aspect of the Tabernacle of David we discussed a few chapters ago. This tent is meant to spread over all that is marked by God for kingdom purpose, according to Amos 9.

As singers, musicians, dancers, and all who minister through sound, what is our apostolic call? I'm about to make it very simple for you:

Matt 28:18-20 *And Jesus came and spoke to them, saying, "All authority is given to me in Heaven and in earth. Therefore go and teach all nations, baptizing them in the name of the Father and of the Son and of* *the Holy Spirit, teaching them to observe all things, whatever I commanded you. And, behold, I am with you all the days until the end of the world. Amen.*

And again:

Luke 10:19-20 *Behold, I give to you authority to tread on serpents and scorpions, and over all the authority of the enemy. And nothing shall by any means hurt you. Yet do not rejoice in this, that the the evil spirits are subject to you, rather rejoice because your names are written in Heaven.*

What sphere are you sent into as a worshiper? Is it church? Is it the streets? The entertainment world? The secular music industry? There should be a sound coming out of you that carries the authority that Jesus has given us through his declaration. Although there seem to be certain things that are ministry-specific in this day and age, we should all have this basic understanding of our apostolic call to show forth the glory of God that shifts and shapes atmospheres, opens blind eyes, pushes back darkness, and causes many to come to his light. Through God, you have the power to penetrate any sphere he sends you into. You have the power to set up, build, and put into motion that which

God has sent you to establish.

Don't be afraid to do what you know to do according to the word of God. There are certain things that Jesus said we'd walk in if we believe. Well I, for one, believe. So I have no doubt that when I step into the role that God has called me to, the apostolic purpose will be fulfilled. I believe that healing can take place. I believe the tone for the prophetic sound can be set. I believe that the glory coming from heaven is greater than any opposition in the air. So that's how I operate. And I've seen incredible things happen.

In the book, *Worship As It Is in Heaven,* by Chuck Pierce and John Dickson, there is a chapter called "The Apostolic Perspective". It's probably my favorite chapter, because it carefully spells out many of the things that hold us back from our call to move apostolically as who we are, and addresses God's desire to use us to redeem what "frustrated creation" has turned into something that is operating in a way that is far less than what it was created to be. Here is a portion of the section subtitled *"Taking Back Music"*:

Apostles look at things differently. While others might look at the corrupted things of the world and run from them to keep from being corrupted by them, apostles look at them and say "That thing belongs to God, and I'm not going to rest until I see it reconciled back to Him." Paul, in Colossians 1:19-20 says, "For it pleased the Father that in Him all the fullness should dwell, and by Him to reconcile all things to Himself, by Him, whether things on earth or things in heaven, having made peace through the blood of His cross." Apostles believe that we are the ones through whom Jesus reconciles all things to the Father. Jesus saves, but it is us that He uses to preach the gospel. In the same way, Jesus reconciles, but it is us that He uses to wrestle the unreconciled to the Father.

When you set foot in any place as one who is releasing sound or movement, desire that everything around is shifted to perfect alignment with the Father. However he uses you, you are there to be a vessel that furthers the plan of God in that place. Ask God to give you a passion for wherever he places your feet, and that his perfect will be performed through you. Know that if he put you there, he will back you up; and you won't have to fear being overcome by whatever is around you if you keep your focus on what he sent you for.

What did he send me for???

Invariably, as soon as we hear things like, "prophesy what God says," or, "focus on why he sent you," or, "be what God has called you to be," that grating question seems to rear its head: *"How do I know what God is saying?"* Let me ease your mind by telling you that you won't have to figure it out. You are a spiritual being doing spiritual things; if you are not resisting God, you'll walk right into whatever and wherever he is leading you. You'll have a dream, or someone will say something that jerks your spirit awake. You'll see a sign or read something that makes God's voice loud, or you may even literally hear God's voice in your ear. An awareness of God and doing what you know to do in obedience to God's word keeps you in a place to receive what he has for you.

There have been times I've walked into a place that I've been invited to minister, and the *only* thing I knew was that I believed God had sent me there. I'd have no idea what I'd say or do. But I've learned to trust the spirit of God in those situations; and he never fails to come through for the people he sent me to. Don't forget, it's not about how well you minister! Your song or dance are not the focus! What is God doing, and is he able to

91

move freely through you? So in those situations, sometimes I won't have a word to say or song to sing until my name is called to minister. Doesn't the word tell us that he fills our mouths? (Luke 12:11-12)

The other side of this is that once you *know* what God has said, do it-- no more, no less. Remember that God's word is alive, whether recorded (logos) or spoken in the moment; therefore to obey and follow through is to enter and/or lead into the best result that God has. When the lord commissioned Joshua (Joshua 6) to march around Jericho, blow horns, and shout, he *sent* him to release a sound that would lead them into triumph. But God gave him specific instructions, and Joshua had to obey by faith, doing only what he was told to do. What made his sound *apostolic* was the fact that God sent him with the authority to carry out his desire-- to tear down strongholds and expand Israel's kingdom according to his promise. So Joshua (not God) moved as an apostle as he moved with God's authority to release the sound, fight, and establish God's purpose.

One thing I say continually is that although I may move apostolically in sound, what I do is still prophetic in nature. In other words, I don't *try* to engage in apostolic worship; I just follow the voice of God in order to connect heaven to earth. David, for example, was a worshiper who was sent in to play music to ease Saul's tormenting spirit. Whether he knew exactly what notes to play or not, we have no way of knowing; but we do know that the distressing spirit would depart whenever David played. He did *what he was sent in to do*, he was aware of the fact that the sound had power, and apparently, that spirit couldn't stay there as the sound went forth. Just as prophetic worship involves an awareness of God's desire, so does apostolic worship.

Hence the reason I don't like to delve too deeply into distinguishing the two!

These days, because the role of apostle had been shunned for so long, the word "apostolic" has partially come to mean that all of the gifts have a place to come forth and be expressed. With this in mind, a good leader will agitate (in the best way possible!) and pull forth the best out of those who are working alongside him or her. When I lead worship, sometimes I'll hear a sound from heaven, and I'll lead the team into it by causing them to express the sound through their gifts. Maybe I'll point to the bass player and give him room to let the deep sound of God come forth, or have a singer or singers sing out a sound that takes us beyond a regular song. Sometimes I'll shape it, and other times I let them form it. Most of the time, it's a dynamic they have never known, and they are introduced to a realm of freedom and heavenly expression that they don't want to live without!

So I reiterate-- the awareness of and submission to God is the key. Jesus, after sending and giving his followers authority to perform miracles and overcome the devil (Luke 10:19-20), warned them not to rejoice in this, but in the fact that their destiny was to dwell with God forever! I believe that if we will stop priding ourselves in our function and trying so hard to understand the intricacies of everything, the wonder and glory of God will become that much brighter to us, in us, and through us.

I read an entry from a worshiper friend of mine, James Nesbit, that I felt was very pertinent to understanding our role as ambassadors in the realm of sound and worship. I'll offer that it brings the connection between the apostolic and prophetic gifts in simple, yet powerful terms; it also shows how vital it is to move beyond what we always do and what we think we know, and move into the power of who God was, is, and will be:

"A year or so ago, while sitting in the back of the room, I watched something profound happening during worship. One moment the room was filled with power, and a few minutes later, there was no power, and then there was another surge of power. What I began to notice was that the power surge was directly related to the language being released by the worship team.

One moment, they were owning the finished work of the cross, and power was everywhere; the next, they were asking him to come and do this or that. In other words, they were asking him to do what he had already done, and it was as if I were watching a power cord being plugged and unplugged from the wall-- it was directly related to the accuracy of the language the team was releasing.

Since that time, I have begun to coin it as 'schizophrenic worship' (a mentality or approch characterized by inconsistent or contradictory elements). I believe that the issue is directly related to flawed or fuzzy eschatology! One minute, we are singing, 'There is a lion on the inside, roaring on the outside,' and the next, we are begging him to come and do something.

The governmental power of 'NOW sound' is that we know he is King, it is finished, and Father is governing through the release of the sound of his sons [and daughters], and we are releasing what he is revealing, right here, right NOW!

The sound of heaven on earth is expanding moment by moment! As you have been reading this, his government and peace have increased throughout the earth, and the zeal of the Lord of Hosts is performing it through the obedient worship of mature sons [and daughters].

Father, everywhere there is 'corroded confusion' in the sound of the sons, we release the power of the blood-covered light of eternal truth concerning the 'IT IS FINISHED' sound of the kingdom purchased by the blood.

Isaiah 9:7 (AMP) Of the increase of his government and of peace there shall be no end, upon the throne of David and over his kingdom, to establish it and to uphold it with justice and with righteousness from the [latter] time forth, even forevermore. The zeal of the Lord of Hosts will perform this.

Isn't that good? Recognizing the power of the one who sent you to release a sound, and knowing his finished work are KEY to the concept of the apostolic sound. Losing the concept of <u>who he is and what he's done</u> is a sure-fire way to foster an atmosphere of powerlessness. But you are sent forth with the majestic, invincible, overcoming, life-giving, tremble-inducing, all consuming, glorious, redeeming power of the Risen Son! Just as he is, so be. Don't take your eyes off of him. I will end this chapter with a brief excerpt from *Moving With Heaven: The Prophetic Worshipers Handbook:*

Earlier, I mentioned that it is our job to facilitate the "ark" of God's presence as we worship Him in song. I believe that the most important thing we can do as worship leaders is to keep our eyes on Jesus. Keep your focus where it matters. I promise that if you do this in whatever environment you are leading, and you remain in a place of watching and seeking Him as you praise and worship Him, you will see what He wants you to see so that you can lead where He wants you to lead. There are times I am not fully aware of whatever darkness is in the atmosphere opposing us, but because I am following after the Lord, something comes out of me that pushes that darkness back.

Doesn't the bible say to draw near to God? It's not

songs or prophecy we draw near to, but God. In the same passage, it says that when we submit to God and resist evil, evil will flee! (James 4:7-8) So again,we keep our focus where it matters...

...The remedy for evil is Jesus. The remedy for death is Jesus. The remedy for sin is Jesus. When in doubt, Jesus. Don't ever forget this.

He is worthy.

Hallelujah, Hallelujah, Hallelujah

The Lord of Hosts, He reigns

Seated on the throne, majestic beauty so bright;

High and lifted up, the train of his robe fills the temple.

And angels cry, "Holy is the Lord!"

So we cry, "Holy is the Lord!"-- the Lord of Hosts.

~ "Lord of Hosts", by James Vincent

VIII. Let Them All Sing

A recurring theme in this book has been that worship does not only occur in church or church settings. Isaiah 43 states that God's sons and daughters were created to worship him. Bringing him glory is our highest call. Whenever I step up to lead in song, I'm looking for how to give the most glory to God through what I do. When I record, I endeavor to not only make good music, but to pour my desire to worship into every note. God is not listening for how awesome we sound. He is looking for the glory that he placed in us to be released outward again.

That takes me to my reason for writing this final chapter. We have to understand that although it would be ideal to have an awesome, beautiful, talented, super-skilled minstrel or singer in our midst, things won't always turn out that way. I've had many ask me to pray with them that they find someone to take that position in their gatherings. Sometimes they even wish ill on my return trip home so that I can live with them forever. Take that up with the wife.

I have visited places, however, where the sound of worship was by no means "up to par" with even the worst musicians. But the hearts of the people to worship and lift up the name of the lord were evident. No one around seemed to care that there were no world-class singers or dancers or instrumentalists; they just wanted to bring glory to the King of Kings! Are you someone who has a home church or group, and are wishing for someone who "really knows how to worship"? Did your worship leader just move and leave your ministry without someone to fill the void? As a son or daughter created to give glory to the lord, I can tell you that you have enough for now.

I can't reiterate enough the fact that God is outside of our minds. We've trained ourselves to think like the world. We believe something has got to look, sound, and act a particular way, according to a societal standard, in order for it to be acceptable. Who told you that your sound wasn't good enough for God? Don't worry about whether or not you sing like Josh Groban or Aretha Franklin. Comparing ourselves among ourselves is like a silent killer in the church; it keeps many gifts dormant and unfruitful. So what I'd like to do is revisit a few key points from the first book,

Moving With Heaven: The Prophetic Worshiper's Handbook, that will help you use what you have to encourage an atmosphere for God's glory to flow freely. But, I'd like you to read it with the understanding that this is not only for the skilled or most talented-- it's for anyone who wants to see the power of God flood their spheres, regions, churches, homes, and wherever they are sent. Let's learn to use what God has given us to see his kingdom come and his will done on earth, just as it is in heaven. Although many baptisms were conducted in the Jordan river, in Acts 8, the Ethiopian simply pointed to some random body of water he and Phillip happened to be passing, and said, "Here's some water. Let's get baptized!" You have what you need; don't be so wrapped up in its form. So here we are:

1. Scripture

Not all of us are fortunate enough to be part of a group that embraces prophetic worship. This exercise is actually advice that I gave to someone I mentor-- he wanted to be able to pray, worship, and prophesy with a group of people that weren't entirely receptive of the spontaneous, prophetic voice. I showed him how to have them prophesy without really telling them that they'd be prophesying.

Take a passage of scripture that applies to a given situation or atmosphere. For instance, if you discern a spirit of shame or abandonment, you can take Ezekiel 16 (look it up) and begin to sing it. You can read it verbatim, or you can pull from the passage to form your own song or repetitive phrase. And if you are the only one there who embraces prophesying, you can just assign the scriptures to those with you, and they are now in agreement with heaven. In many of the worship workshops I conduct, I encourage everyone to sing and not simply speak. It helps to put everyone on the same level, no matter whether someone sings on or off-pitch or has a beautiful tone or not.

In your personal time, find scriptures that pertain to different situations, such as joy, despair, healing, sacrifice, etc. Whatever causes these scriptures to come alive in you, go with it. For myself, I find that meditating for a few days on one scripture really helps, and it comes alive in me when I use it musically. Get on your instrument and/or sing it out over and over. And have fun with it... It doesn't have to feel like work.

2. Worship/prayer group
Years ago, I was part of a home gathering whose focus

was ascending in worship. Someone would play an instrument, we worshiped God with songs everyone knew. Then, there would be a time that we'd transition into a kind of spontaneous song that led into the direction for prophecy. This wasn't all necessarily scripture; it was mostly inspired by discerning heaven. In this group, everyone had to sing their prophetic word, whether they were singers or not. I thought that was pretty brilliant; and for much of the time, the instrumentalist is still playing whatever he feels. Sometimes the music would speak, sometimes the voices would sing, and sometimes the voices would prophesy an interpretation of the music.

Understand that we weren't perhaps always interpreting correctly what we discerned, but the good thing about an atmosphere like this was that it was a "safe" place to make mistakes and learn. As long as God is the center, He is faithful to release and correct what needs to be corrected.

Everyone in the room was encouraged to be a part. One thing that I began to notice was that after a few weeks or months, the ones who were typically shy or insecure in the beginning would, little by little, begin releasing spontaneous, prophetic songs. (See the first book for an explanation on the difference between spontaneous and prophetic.)

3. Sing your prayers

This is actually my favorite thing in my personal time. I find that music surpasses so many different boundaries, physical and spiritual. When I sing my prayers, I find myself going beyond a realm of praying from my head and entering into a supernatural agreement with the realm of heaven. I begin to pray God's desire, and I suddenly see images before me or in my mind that cause me to know how and what to pray. In that moment, everything I look at, I am able to interpret through prophetic eyes. I even begin to receive accurate words from God for others. I'm sure some expert in metaphysics could explain this in better depth, but all I know is that I connect better personally through song.

Sometimes you may use words, other times you may sing in tongues or just release a wordless melody. Whatever you do, let that agreement begin to form in you until you see what God is releasing.

It's good to do this with children as well. I've done this with my children, and it becomes something fun for them, it helps to develop their creativity, and breaks off some of the self-consciousness that so many encounter when moving into prophesying.

4. Desire to Prophesy

I wouldn't consider this an exercise in the same context of the previous ones, but as prophetic worshipers, it behooves us to want to hear God and speak forth His heart. Pray and pray again, seek and seek again for this gift to awaken inside of you. And open your mouth! One way evil works is to shut the mouth of the prophets so that a people remain in poverty and famine. Do not allow spirits of timidity and fear to cause you to shrink back from prophesying. Let that fire rise up in you as it did in Jeremiah (Jer 20:9), and you won't be able to keep silent! Ask for it! You do not have to carry the "title" of prophet in order to move in prophecy. A great book on this is *Prophet Arise*, by John Eckhardt.

Believe that you are a spiritual being. If you are working to keep a <u>clear conscience, and keeping things before the lord in your life</u>, you should have the confidence to know that the lord is able to use you however he desires. When you see something in the spirit, whether it be a "random thought" or even something physical that is being highlighted to you, know that sometimes Holy Spirit will use those things to make you know what he is saying to you. One example of this is that one night, I was leading worship at a Hispanic gathering. As I sang, I suddenly felt something in my foot. Because I trust God's spirit, I knew that the lord wanted to heal feet. So I spoke it forth, and prophesied God's will in the hearing of everyone there. My goal was not to gain confirmation or affirmation; it was to speak God's will. I continued to sing after that. The following week, the leader who was over that gathering let me know that multiple people testified that their feet had been healed that night! Hallelujah! I could have written off that feeling in my foot as some coincidental, random event, but I chose to see it as God's spirit communicating with my spirit. We are spiritual beings.

Keep your heart open to prophesy as you worship. What is heaven's desire *right now?* We really can discern and know what the Lord wants to say and do at a certain time. Take time to pray again that all of your senses awaken to the purposes of God in your atmosphere. One of our main goals in prophetic worship is to connect heaven to earth, and the most effective times in song are when we are actually doing what heaven is doing.

5. Discern and declare

I did a certain teaching once, and many of the people I taught were amazed at the realization that in every atmosphere, there is some spiritual force opposing the worship of the one true God. The enemy works to scatter and divide us and divide our focus in order to throw the plan of God through us into disarray. As prophetic worshipers, we should be aware that we are gifted to dispel whatever darkness is coming against our worship *through our prophetic declaration.* Remember, the declaration can be formed in such a way that everyone can join in and repeat it with you. I find this to be most effective, because it causes us to all be in one accord as we prophesy together.

In Ezekiel 37 (the passage about the army of dry bones), the Lord showed Ezekiel the dejected state of the hearts of the people of Israel, and then said, *"Therefore prophesy..."* If you ever discern anything in your atmosphere, know that you have authority in the

107

spirit to somehow address it through God's leading. By "somehow", I mean that you may not necessarily use exact, direct language in terms of what you are accomplishing in the spirit. Sometimes, if I see that there is faithlessness in the air, I won't necessarily say, "There is faithlessness here, and it must go NOW!" , but I might say, "Don't you know that nothing is too hard for God? Lift up your eyes and see your help! He is unable to fail!" The level of faith rises, faithlessness diminishes. The enemy loses.

6. Don't aim for perfectionn

Yes, that's right, I spelled it rong to bother some of you fokls who like everything to be perfeck. As we said earlier, God explains that perfection is when your heart is completely bent towards him (and you are cleansed by the blood of the Lamb of God). I know... you've got a picture in your mind of what things are supposed to look and sound like; I go through it very often. However, I have become very careful not to let my expectations overtake the will of God. As a matter of fact, the goal I aim towards is to remain true to what heaven has released to me; or keep *the integrity of the sound*. Although there are slightly different angles some of us come from within this-- for example, I write and compose music-- in the end, there is a message or act that the lord wants to convey. And yes, there will be some things that will need to grow and become better, but have patience to allow those things room to improve. Remember, we don't have every piece to the puzzle. Let God be who he is; otherwise we forget that he is not some formula that we have to figure out all of the ingredients to.

I'd like to briefly add that if you typically use a CD or some type of recording for worship when you gather, please be sure not to shut down the new song that may want to come forth out of you or someone else. Make room for the spontaneous sound of heaven in your midst. Sometimes you won't need music at all. When the the lord gives me an assignment to sing over someone or some place, I go with only my voice. The new song flows through our obedience and willingness to allow God to show himself through us, not our skill or equipment. Make room.

In many of the epic movies we love to watch, many times, the hero needs to attain some weapon or trinket, locate some person, or unravel some kind of mystery in order to attain what he needs to achieve victory. But as we read the word, we see that many times the Lord points out that we already have what we need. Let's not think the way the world has trained us to think; lets conform our minds to the will of heaven, so that we can see and discern correctly. So what if you sing off-pitch. God's ears are better than ours. And if your voice belongs to him, what he hears is beautiful.

Conclusion

I looked out of the window as I sat on a plane during one of my many travels. I always appreciate the view when the clouds are set in their unique patterns, or when the stars are so clear and bright. This particular day, however, the view was especially magnificent, as the sun shone in the background, creating a beautiful shimmer across the tops of the colorful clouds in a fading sky. I beckoned to my wife to enjoy the view with me. Then I became overwhelmed. I began to weep and thank the Lord for allowing me to witness such marvelous beauty. My heart overflowed with the desire to *"todah"* and *"barak"* him.

God is all around us, and as his children, we are created to hear, witness, and connect with him wherever we are. He is so much more than a church service, outside of the focal points of our ministries, gifts, or brands. His words (logos) are beyond words on a page; they are alive and still being recorded to this day. He is infinitely beyond our ability to study him; we simply need to acknowledge him and allow him to place us within the "allness" of who he is. And it's in this place of love, truth, and submission that we find the ability to move with him however he desires, just as Jesus did when he walked the earth.

God is… And he desires to *be* through you.

Notes

Notes

Notes

Made in the USA
San Bernardino, CA
28 February 2017